Chicago Tribune

Hawkeytown

Chicago Blackhawks' Run
for the 2010 Stanley Cup

Chicago Tribune

Tony W. Hunter, Publisher
Gerould W. Kern, Editor
R. Bruce Dold, Editorial Page Editor
Bill Adee, Vice President/Digital
Jane Hirt, Managing Editor
Joycelyn Winnecke, Associate Editor
Peter Kendall, Deputy Managing Editor

Hawkey town

Chicago Blackhawks' Run for the 2010 Stanley Cup

Mike Kellams, Editor

Steve Rosenberg, Photo Editor

Chuck Burke and Joan Cairney, Art Directors

Christine Bruno and Kathy Celer, Imagers

Tom Carkeek, Copy Editor

This book is available in quantity at special discounts for your group or organization. For further information, contact:

Triumph Books
542 South Dearborn Street
Suite 750
Chicago, Illinois 60605
(312) 939-3330
Fax (312) 663-3557
www.triumphbooks.com

Printed in U.S.A.
ISBN: 978-1-60078-528-3

Front and back cover photos:
Nuccio DiNuzzo

The Chicago Tribune's Stanley Cup photographers: Nuccio DiNuzzo, Brian Cassella and Scott Strazzante.
JOHN MARSCHITZ

Bathed in light and basking in the roar of the crowd, Brian Campbell and Troy Brouwer take the ice before the Hawks' 7–4 win in Game 5 of the Stanley Cup finals.
SCOTT STRAZZANTE

CONTENTS

After playing much of the season in the shadow of Cristobal Huet, the Hawks put the spotlight on Antti Niemi near the end of the season and throughout their playoff run. BRIAN CASSELLA

David Haugh,
Chicago Tribune
10

Steve Rosenbloom,
Chicago Tribune
14

The 2009-10 Season
16

The Profiles:
Quenneville
18

Toews
38

Kane
44

Niemi
50

Byfuglien
56

Keith
62

Hossa
68

The Fans
72

The Stats
78

The Playoffs
80

Nashville
82

Vancouver
92

Conference Final:
San Jose
102

Stanley Cup Final:
Philadelphia
112

The skyline on the night the Hawks
won it: June 9, 2010. CHRIS SWEDA

Per tradition, the contest had already started between anthem singer Jim Cornelison and the crowd to see who was loudest. Everybody won.
BRIAN CASSELLA

It's just like new times

By David Haugh

His dark suit soaked with a mixture of beer and bubbly, John McDonough finally walked out of the frat party the Blackhawks dressing room had become amid the Stanley Cup title celebration.

"Where's the team bus? Let's go!" McDonough said as he whisked down a hallway inside Philadelphia's Wachovia Center.

He already had taken the wildest ride of his life, and now he was in a hurry to head home to Chicago, where he knew better than anybody the satisfaction that awaited the Hawks.

"I'm thrilled for our fans, all those who had to wait ... because if there is anybody in sports who knows what it's like to wait, it's me," McDonough said with a smirk.

He wasn't bragging.

McDonough can relate to Blackhawks faithful whose 49-year wait ended when Patrick Kane scored the game-winner in a 4-3 overtime victory over the Flyers. McDonough symbolizes more than the hospital-corners operation the Blackhawks organization has become. At heart he is a long-suffering Chicago sports fan, which is redundant, and he has the scar tissue to prove it.

He worked in the Cubs front office for 24 years, ascending through the ranks to team president. At Wrigley Field, waiting 49 years for a championship is a good start. So McDonough, perhaps even more than Hawks Chairman Rocky Wirtz, experienced the relief a city felt every bit as much as the joy.

That's why when the entire organization was on the ice for the Stanley Cup trophy presentation late in the night of June 9, 2010, it felt to McDonough like Hawks fans had endured a wait even longer than 49 years. It felt like more than lifting one sports franchise's burden. It felt better than just One Goal being realized.

It felt like Chicago's victory as much as it was the Blackhawks'.

"I have been working in sports in Chicago for 30 years, and the feeling, the exhilaration, I feel tonight is indescribable," McDonough said, his voice heavy with emotion. "It's by far the greatest night I've had."

It's easily the most impressive renovation project in Chicago sports history.

The Hawks remind me of the Internet.

It's impossible for many people, especially those in their 20s, to imagine life without Google, Facebook or Twitter. How did we find phone numbers and maps and restaurant or movie reviews before the World Wide Web? It seems long ago, another era, a time when things didn't come as easily and there was always a good reason for something getting in the way.

The same thing can be said about the Hawks before McDonough and Wirtz arrived within a month of each other in 2007.

Seeing the way they have become the class of the NHL, on and off the ice, it's hard to remember when the United Center was empty for Hawks games and the hockey team was inept. Those memories seem like ones from a bygone era. They aren't.

That was earlier this decade, before the team televised home games, before they drafted Jona-

With encouragement from Tony Esposito (35), Bobby Hull (good ole No. 9) and Stan Mikita (21) twirl around the ice during the regular season. The Hawks welcomed back their legends, then welcomed back the Cup. NUCCIO DINUZZO

It felt like more than lifting one sports franchise's burden. It felt better than just One Goal being realized. It felt like Chicago's victory as much as it was the Blackhawks'.

than Toews and Patrick Kane, before they hired McDonough as team president on Nov. 20, 2007 — and, yes, before Bill Wirtz died Sept. 26, 2007.

This Blackhawks rebirth began with a death. It's a reality that can't be ignored when documenting history that's been made.

Almost immediately, Rocky Wirtz put the Hawks on TV, reached out to fans and improved conditions for players so much that veterans such as Marian Hossa and John Madden would target the Hawks during free agency. Almost immediately, the Hawks spent money to sign and keep elite players.

Would any of this have happened before 2007?

I know the answer. I also know it's hard to remember what the Hawks were like way back then, and it figures to become even harder for a new culture of Blackhawks fans with every victory celebration.

David Haugh is a Chicago Tribune columnist.

Antti Niemi lost his mask but kept his head against the Flyers in the Stanley Cup finals. BRIAN CASSELLA

It's happy hour; Rocky's serving

By Steve Rosenbloom

Young Blackhawks captain Jonathan Toews dramatically rammed the Stanley Cup skyward. The longest failure streak in the NHL had its exclamation point.

Toews then made the slickest of moves, passing the silver chalice to a heroic Marian Hossa, who had played in three straight finals and lost the first two. The championship ritual was on. Player after player took the Cup and made the skate of indescribable joy.

Finally, Hawks Chairman Rocky Wirtz got a turn to raise hockey's Holy Grail to the heavens on June 9, 2010. Cut. Print it. There's your perfect ending to the "Rocky Hallelujah Picture Show."

The Hawks were champions.

That's a sentence I never thought I'd write and probably wouldn't if it weren't for Rocky Wirtz.

I've often said I love hockey but hate what Rocky's father, Bill, did to it on Madison Street. I didn't believe Rocky's dad wanted to do what it took to win the Cup. That cost money. I recall Bill Wirtz saying he wouldn't want his family to spend like Mike Ilitch's family did in Detroit, where, by the way, the Red Wings won and won and won and ...

Bill Wirtz died in September 2007. Rocky took over on Oct. 5, his 55th birthday. Almost immediately, the sins of the father were righted by the son.

One of Rocky's first moves was to put home games on television, an act his father would have viewed as heresy but one that dragged the 19th-Century organ-I-zation into the new millennium.

Next, stunningly, he hired Cubs President and marketing master John McDonough to make the Hawks relevant — and champions. Rocky's willingness to spend money to make money allowed McDonough to strengthen the business side of the franchise, eventually putting every home game on television and selling more tickets than any NHL team.

More importantly, it allowed McDonough to strengthen the hockey side, starting with luring Scotty Bowman from the rival Wings to serve as Hockey Oracle.

There would be difficult times. Replacing Hawks legend Denis Savard with Joel Quenneville as coach and removing longtime Hawks employee Dale Tallon for Bowman's son, Stan, as general manager hurt on a personal level but reflected Rocky's belief that he had to allow people to do the jobs he'd hired them to do.

And, oh, how they did their jobs. Better than anyone in the NHL this season.

All of them. Individually and collectively. On the ice and off it.

But success starts at the top. And good for the man on top of the Hawks franchise.

Rocky Wirtz smiles often and laughs easily. There is no attitude about him. If anything, he personifies giddiness, more cheerleader than chairman.

Now he has been rewarded on both fronts. His family's 49-year wait is over. The Hawks got to tip the Cup. As the man who also oversees the family's liquor distributorship wryly noted, "It's been a long time between drinks."

Just guessing that all of Hockey Chicago would be happy to buy.

Steve Rosenbloom is a Chicago Tribune columnist.

Hawks chairman Rocky Wirtz hoists the Stanley Cup after his team clinched its first title in 49 years. BRIAN CASSELLA

Ben Eager clears out
Detroit's Todd Bertuzzi
in the Hawks' 5-4 loss to
the Red Wings in March.
SCOTT STRAZZANTE

The 2009-10 Season

PROFILE **Joel Quenneville**

By David Haugh

He always prepared for a quiet, secure life after hockey.

Near the end of a 13-year NHL career as a trusty, no-frills defenseman, Joel Quenneville spent summers in Hartford, where he played seven of those seasons, selling securities for a local brokerage firm.

Being a broker felt safe. But being a coach felt right.

It was 1990. The Whalers had just traded Quenneville to his fifth NHL team, the Capitals, who banished him to their American Hockey League team

in Baltimore after just nine games. But a funny thing happened to Quenneville on his way to NHL retirement after 803 games in the league: For the first time, Quenneville the Player seriously considered the transition to Quenneville the Coach.

"I was 32, and that year in Baltimore helped me think I'd like to stay in the game if I could," said Quenneville, now 51 and leading the Blackhawks.

Quenneville was hired as a player-coach with the St. John's Maple Leafs in the AHL as an assistant under Marc Crawford, currently head coach of the Stars.

Quenneville moved on in 1992 to coach the Springfield Indians of the AHL. That's where he

what he wanted to grow up to do, and now here was the ultimate prize right there in front of us," she said. "To see Joel's face ... I get goose bumps right now just talking about it. It was just an overwhelming experience for him and everybody."

The Cup was confirmation to Quenneville that when he trusts his gut — as he did entering coaching — good things happen.

That inner confidence that everything will work out, the outer strength players and fans see from Quenneville, didn't always exist.

It was Dec. 29, 1979, and Quenneville was a promising defenseman in his second season with a Maple Leafs team that drafted him in the first round in 1978. But the Leafs traded him to the then-Colorado Rockies.

"You learn a lot going through something like that," Quenneville said. "That was a tough trade."

The entire experience developed within Quenneville a code for dealing with players. He never wants one of his guys to be blindsided like he was as a naïve 21-year-old shaken to his core.

"You learn that you want to let them know where they stand," Quenneville said. "It's never personal. That's the way it is. Try to make sure everybody's happy and know what is expected. In our business, lay it out there, be yourself, expect the best.

"I don't like secrets."

And it's no secret that Quenneville exudes gruffness, a perception that cracks up the Quennevilles' teenage children.

Several nights ago, Quenneville was enjoying his first night at home after more than a week in California when he encountered a question tougher than any reporter had posed this postseason. His wife had just turned down daughter Anna's request when Anna appealed to her father via text because, well, in hockey terms, the Quenneville kids know from experience how the home refs call it.

"I'll say, 'No, no, no.' But they know they can go to Dad," Elizabeth said. "I won't say he's a pushover, but he's the one who will give in quickest."

Inside the glass, the suburban softie transforms into a hardened hockey coach whose style has complemented his strategy, whose legacy is waiting to be written, whether he likes it or not.

"One thing about coaching: It's all about team, it's not about me," Quenneville said. "I don't need attention. I don't care about that. It's about the guys. They're the ones that do it, and that's the way I like it. My job is keep the team organized the best we can and maximize every single guy so they're out there playing the best they can play. ... Walking to the United Center every day is a unique thing, and I feel fortunate.

was when Crawford became the head coach in Quebec and offered Quenneville a job on his staff — his avenue back into the NHL.

When the Nordiques moved to Denver to become the Colorado Avalanche, Quenneville went with them, a move that looked like the best of his career after the Avalanche won the Cup in 1996.

As is hockey tradition, Quenneville took the Cup home for a day. The Quenneville family threw a party, Lord Stanley's trophy the guest of honor. Quenneville's wife Elizabeth never will forget her husband's reaction.

A franchise record-setting regular season

By Chris Kuc

The odyssey that was the Blackhawks' 2009-10 regular season began with a shootout loss thousands of miles from Chicago to an opponent they rarely play and ended with an overtime defeat to their arch-rivals at home. In between was a wild ride throughout North America that featured thrills, chills and spills and ultimately a franchise-record number of wins and the fond memories that came with them.

October: 8-4-1

In a road trip like no other, the Hawks opened the season in Europe with two games against the Florida Panthers in Helsinki, Finland. In what might have been a bit of foreshadowing for the rest of the season, veteran goaltender Cristobal Huet suffered the loss in the opener and Antti Niemi—who was awarded the backup job just days earlier—earned the win in Game 2.

After dropping their North American opener to the Red Wings at the United Center on Oct. 8, 2009, the Hawks won four consecutive games and included in that was the first magical moment of '09-10.

On Oct. 12, the Hawks were thoroughly thrashed in the first period by the Flames and trailed 5-0 after one period. Perhaps sparked by a chorus of boos from the home faithful, the Hawks mounted a rally for the ages and equaled the biggest comeback in NHL history to stun the Flames 6-5 on Brent Seabrook's goal 26 seconds into overtime.

"Pretty amazing game," Hawks coach Joel Quenneville said. "From the worst to as good as you can get. It was a dramatic turn."

Two more victories followed and then two loss-es—the latter setback a costly one as team captain Jonathan Toews suffered a concussion following a devastating open-ice hit from Canucks defenseman Willie Mitchell and missed six games.

November: 8-2-2
Season: 16-6-3

The month started on a down note as without their leader, the Hawks lost the first two games in November before sweeping a four-game homestand prior to the annual Circus Trip. The good times continued to roll as they barreled through the Canadian portion of the journey, including a 7-1 shellacking of the Flames on Nov. 19 at the Saddledome.

After a spirited 30-save effort by Niemi resulted in a 1-0 shutout over the Canucks, the Hawks rolled into San Jose riding a seven-game winning streak. Even they couldn't have expected what happened next.

In perhaps their most dominating performance of the season, the Hawks tore apart the Sharks 7-2 on Nov. 25 on the strength of three short-handed

Continued on Page 25

Patrick Sharp's game winner in a 3-2 shootout victory over Colorado in November helped the Hawks to a 5-4 record in shootouts during the season. SCOTT STRAZZANTE

In their first regular season matchup since the Hawks eliminated the Canucks in the 2009 playoffs, Vancouver's Willie Mitchell puts a hard hit on Hawks captain Jonathan Toews. Vancouver won this October game, 3-2. NUCCIO DINUZZO

The United Center crowd erupts with Jonathan Toews as the Hawks celebrate Patrick Kane's first-period goal against Colorado in November. SCOTT STRAZZANTE

goals, including one by winger Marian Hossa, who was making his season and Hawks debut following shoulder surgery. The loss was the first home regulation loss of the season for San Jose.

"It was a great test and we passed this test," Hossa said. "We just proved we can play against anybody."

The winning streak came to a halt two days later at the hands of the Ducks and the road trip concluded with a 2-1 shootout loss to the Kings. The trip was a rousing success as they finished 4-1-1.

December: 11-4-0
Season: 27-10-3

After splitting the first two games of the month, Niemi began asserting himself in a bid to work his way into the Hawks' goaltending mix. The Finnish netminder was brilliant in a 2-1 overtime victory over the defending champion Penguins on Dec. 5, 2009 in Pittsburgh. Niemi stopped 32 of 33 shots and Kris Versteeg scored in overtime to end it.

A five-game homestand mid-month meant the piling up of points as the Hawks won the first four before dropping a 3-2 heartbreaker to the Sharks on Dec. 22 at the United Center. They outshot San Jose 47-14 but fell to a dominating performance by Sharks goalie Evgeni Nabokov.

They didn't let the difficult defeat bother them, however, as the next night Niemi put together a 33-save, 3-0 blanking of the Red Wings in Detroit.

A 4-1 finish to the month included a 5-1 thrashing of the Devils and Hall-of-Fame goalie Martin Brodeur on New Year's Eve at the UC. Twelve Hawks forwards scored in the game to set a franchise record.

January: 10-4-1
Season: 37-14-4

Four consecutive victories to start the month had the Hawks flying high with a five-game winning streak and when they took a 5-1 lead into the third period against the Wild in Minnesota on Jan. 9, 2010, win No. 6 didn't appear too far behind. Instead, the Hawks wilted and suffered their most gut-wrenching loss of the season when the Wild scored four times in the third and won it in a shootout.

A 3-1 loss to the Ducks at home the next night added to the misery, but the Hawks weren't down for long. With the longest road trip of the season looming, they dropped the Blue Jackets 3-0 on Jan. 14 before heading to Columbus for the first of an eight-game trip.

In what may have been the best harbinger for

Continued on Page 27

Kris Versteeg controls the puck from the Capitals' David Steckel in March. JOSE M. OSORIO

the success the rest of the way, the Hawks went 5-3 on the 7,800-mile trek, including wins in Calgary and Edmonton.

Sandwiched between was a 5-1 loss to the Canucks in Vancouver and the escalation of the rivalry between the teams. Late in the first period, Ryan Kesler of the Canucks—apparently still angered by a hit during the previous postseason—challenged Hawks winger Andrew Ladd to a fight. The bout didn't last long as Ladd drilled Kesler with a quick punch that effectively ended the skirmish. Afterward, Kesler called Ladd "a coward" and the bad feelings between the teams had grown.

"It seems like he had a lot of stuff bottled up," Ladd said. "He was talking lots before but didn't really say much after the fight."

A showdown between the NHL's top two teams resulted in a 4-3 overtime Hawks win over the Sharks in San Jose. The trip ended two nights later following a cross-country flight that left the ragged Hawks vulnerable and they fell 4-2 to Carolina.

February: 4-1-1
Season: 41-15-5

The 15-day break for the Olympics meant a light month for all but the six Hawks headed to Vancouver for the 2010 Winter Games. Before the stoppage, the Hawks dropped two contests but then won four consecutive, including the final three in shootouts.

The Olympic break

While the rest of the Hawks grabbed some well-deserved rest, Jonathan Toews, Duncan Keith, Brent Seabrook, Patrick Kane, Marian Hossa and Tomas Kopecky donned their respective countries sweaters and participated in the Olympics. After Slovakia's Hossa and Kopecky fell short of a medal, Toews, Keith and Seabrook of Canada clashed with the United States' Kane in an epic gold-medal contest. Canada skated to a 3-2 overtime victory and Toews showcased his skills to the world with a goal and seven assists during the tournament and was named the most valuable forward.

"You don't want this to slip away because it's an unbelievable feeling and something that maybe comes once in a lifetime," Toews said.

Said Kane, who's dynamic play made him the most dangerous forward on the ice: "You come here and you think of the feeling that it's going to be winning gold, but you never really get it. You have to wait another four years to have a chance at it so it stings a bit."

Continued on Page 35

Blackhawk

4
JERRY SLOAN
1966-1976
10
BOB LOVE
1968-1976
82
8
Four Seasons
HEATING & AIR CONDITIONING
NHL.COM
HARRIS
WARRIOR
BAUER

Olympians

A break in the season to represent
the United States, Canada and Slovakia
at the Winter Olympics in Vancouver

Hawks Olympians included Tomas Kopecky and Marian Hossa of Slovakia, silver medal winner Patrick Kane of the United States and gold medal winners Jonathan Toews, Duncan Keith and Brent Seabrook of Canada. SCOTT STRAZZANTE

Tomas Kopecky, Slovakia

Patrick Kane, United States

Marian Hossa, Slovakia

Duncan Keith, Canada

Jonathan Toews, Canada

Brent Seabrook, Canada

At Vancouver's Olympics, Patrick Kane's first of two goals against Finland gave the United States a 4-0 lead.
The Americans beat the Finns 6-1 in the semifinals but lost the gold medal game to Canada, 3-2. NUCCIO DINUZZO

PORTRAITS: E. JASON WAMBSGANS

Canada's Jonathan Toews likes the weight of gold around his neck.
NUCCIO DINUZZO

The faces of the Hawks franchise — Patrick Kane and Jonathan Toews — meet after the U.S.'s 5-3 win over Canada in pool play. NUCCIO DINUZZO

March: 6-7-2
Season: 47-22-7

In the Hawks' only sub-.500 month, they seemed to succumb to the dog days of the season.

Two noteworthy—and painful—incidents in consecutive games had an impact as the Hawks were in a battle with the Sharks for the top spot in the Western Conference.

During a March 14 game at the United Center against the Capitals, defenseman Brian Campbell was seriously injured when he was checked into the boards by Washington superstar Alex Ovechkin. Campbell broke a rib and his collarbone and was lost to the Hawks until the first round of the playoffs. Ovechkin, meanwhile, was suspended for two days for the reckless hit which he downplayed by saying "just pushed" Campbell.

"I think the intent was there," Campbell said. "If the intent is there, I don't think you can really say you didn't mean to do anything."

The next game March 17, defenseman Brent Seabrook took a vicious hit from former teammate and friend James Wisniewski and suffered a concussion causing him to miss two games.

"For 'Wiz' to come from the blueline the way he did and leave his feet and go right for my head, I don't think is fair for any player and especially not a friend," Seabrook said.

After the incidents, the Hawks lost four of their next seven games and needed a late-season push to keep pace with San Jose.

April: 5-0-1
Season: 52-22-8

When the new month rolled around, the Hawks did just that as they won the first five games of April to run their winning streak to six. It set up a showdown with the Wings on April 11 at the United Center in the final regular-season game of 2009-10. A win would have meant the Hawks would finish at the top of conference. Instead, Detroit broke Hawks fans' hearts with a 3-2 victory in overtime and the Hawks finished second in the West.

"We came up a bit short," Kane said. "Overall, how can you argue about our year? We set a lot of franchise records."

After the dust settled on the season, the Hawks had claimed their first division title since 1992-93 and set a team record for victories in a season with 52 and points with 112.

Patrick Kane looks happy surrounded by Blues. He would have been happier if his shot had not been stopped in the Hawks' 3-2 loss in February. SCOTT STRAZZANTE

Dustin Byfuglien mixes it up with Anaheim's Troy Bodie in the Hawks' 5-2 win in January. SCOTT STRAZZANTE

PROFILE Jonathan Toews

By Philip Hersh

It seemed incongruous to have a Jonathan Toews jersey draped over the Michael Jordan statue outside the United Center before the Stanley Cup finals.

Jordan's brilliance was spectacular. Toews' is subtle.

Jordan's personality is outsized. Toews' goes comfortably on his 6-foot-2, 210-pound body.

There's a reason teammates began to call Toews "Captain Serious" almost as soon as the "C" went on his sweater two years ago.

He was just 20 then, the third-youngest captain in NHL history.

And the nickname was a perfect fit.

"I've taken a lot of heat from some of my teammates for being so serious," Toews told the Tribune's Judy Hevrdejs in December. "But it's all good.

"And I guess it's been my nature. I think my parents are both serious people who value hard work and not taking anything you've been given for granted, and that's the way it's always been."

So it's no surprise Toews is one of the best two-way forwards in the league, one who finds back-checking and goal scoring equally satisfying.

Or that Vancouver coach Alain Vigneault accused Toews of being more down and dirty than Dustin Byfuglien in harassing Canucks goalie Roberto Luongo during the second-round playoff series.

Subtleties come in many forms for an NHL player.

So does obvious brilliance, like the three goals and two assists Toews had in the first two periods of Game 4 against the Canucks.

Playing on a checking line for Team Canada at the Olympics, Toews came home with both a gold medal and the honor of having been named the tournament's top forward. He also had the best plus/minus rating in the Olympics.

"His Olympics probably illustrates his whole career, how it's gone," Hawks coach Joel Quenneville said. "He got better and better as the tournament went on."

Playing on the Hawks' top line throughout the season, Toews had 25 goals and 43 assists and was a plus-22. (He has had a positive rating in each of his three NHL seasons.) Killing penalties and working the power play, he averaged 20 minutes of ice time per game during the regular season, most by any Hawks forward.

Going into the Cup finals, Toews was the league's leading scorer during the playoffs.

In December, the Hawks signed the native of Winnipeg to a five-year contract extension worth a reported $31.5 million. So there should be no problem making the mortgage payments on his 2,700-square-foot, 30th-floor condo with commanding views of downtown Chicago.

And, off in the distance, a jersey placement that his stature, if not his style, commands.

At 22, "Captain Serious" is among the NHL's youngest captains ever, a respected leader in Chicago and on Canada's Olympic team.
SCOTT STRAZZANTE

Dustin Byfuglien gives it a whirl with most of the St. Louis Blues. E. JASON WAMBSGANS

Just 1:55 after the Blues had taken the lead over the Hawks in April, Duncan Keith scored in a blur to even the score in a game Chicago won 6-5. E. JASON WAMBSGANS

PROFILE **Patrick Kane**

By Philip Hersh

For Patrick Kane, this was to be another season of burnishing a reputation as one of hockey's young superstars until it took on a fine sheen.

But his off-ice exploits, which couldn't be glossed over, made him seem like bad-boy actor Charlie Sheen.

There was the August altercation with a Buffalo cabdriver that led to misdemeanor charges against Kane. The charges were dropped when he pleaded guilty to disorderly conduct, a non-criminal violation.

There was a photo of Kane and teammate Adam Burish in blackface, dressed as Chicago Bulls for a Halloween party.

Then, barely a month after signing a five-year contract extension worth a reported $31 million, there was a photo of a shirtless Kane drinking in the back of a Vancouver limousine with shirtless teammates John Madden and Kris Versteeg and three unidentified (and fully clothed) young women.

Kane finally realized that even if he is younger than many college seniors, he had to stop acting like an extra in "Animal House."

"I've had a couple of incidents, obviously," Kane said after the limo photos surfaced. "It's something

I'm going to have to learn. I'm 21 years old, but it's probably time to grow up a little bit."

On the ice, Kane showed his continued development from 18-year-old first draft choice phenom to highly productive veteran:

■ He was the youngest member of the silver-medal 2010 U.S. Olympic hockey team, for which he scored four points in the medal round and made an all-guts backcheck to stop Sidney Crosby on a breakaway in the championship game.

■ He became the youngest player in franchise history to reach 200 career points. "It means a lot," Kane said. "Coming in as a pretty hyped-up first overall pick, you want to come in and live up to that hype."

■ He led all U.S.-born NHL players with 88 points, ranking ninth overall, and had the first positive plus-minus rating (+16) of his three NHL seasons.

■ He scored the short-handed goal that may have saved the Hawks' Cup hopes with 13.6 seconds left in regulation in Game 5 of the opening playoff series against Nashville. The Hawks won in overtime, sending them to Nashville with a 3-2 series lead for the eventual clinching victory.

"I don't even remember the game, to be honest," Kane said. "I just remember us winning."

That's the winning image Kane wants to project.

While not being distracted by incidents off the ice, Patrick Kane, mouthpiece agape, came into his own as one of the league's emerging stars.
SCOTT STRAZZANTE

While Boston's finest watch, the Hawks' Andrew Ladd and Patrick Sharp battle each other for the puck in Chicago's 5-4 shootout win in December. CHRIS SWEDA

Los Angeles King Rich Clune find himself where much of the league ends up: Wanting to punch Hawk instigator Adam Burish during the Hawks' 3-2 overtime win in March. CHRIS SWEDA

PROFILE **Antti Niemi**

By Philip Hersh

To understand Antti Niemi, who throws around words as if they were manhole covers, you need to know Finnish character.

Merete Mazzarella, professor emerita of Nordic literature at the University of Helsinki, illustrates it with a joke about two Finns who go out drinking. They sit in silence for a long time until the drinks arrive, and then one raises his glass and says, "Cheers!" But he is chastised by his companion, who replies, "Have we come to drink or to chat?"

"Main themes when Finnish character is described have always been shyness, taciturnity and obstinate perseverance," Mazzarella said.

Sound like a Blackhawks goalie we (don't) know?

The only flash about Niemi comes in the lightning movement of his pads. Teammates have nicknamed Niemi the Octopus, for his legs are so flexible and quick in stopping shots it sometimes seems he has eight.

It is a personality often linked to spending long winters on isolated farms or in small villages, where social interactions are limited.

That does not hold for Niemi: His hometown, Vantaa, with a population of nearly 200,000, is the fourth-largest city in Finland and part of metropolitan Helsinki.

"Maybe I try not to be fiery," he has said.

Niemi played from age 17 to 21 on elite junior and senior teams in Vantaa, then moved for three seasons to a Finnish first division team in Lahti, a city of 100,000. The Lahti Pelicans finished 12th, 10th and sixth in the 14-team league in Niemi's stay there, which ended when the Blackhawks signed him as a free agent in May 2008.

Having played just three NHL games last season, the 26-year-old Niemi was seen this season as the backup to pricey Cristobal Huet after the Hawks let Nikolai Khabibulin leave in free agency. Niemi played in only 18 of the Hawks' first 57 games and did not become the starter for good until March 28, after Huet had allowed seven goals in the previous game.

Despite that, he tied for third in the league with seven shutouts and added two in the first round of the playoffs. Niemi allowed just one and two goals, respectively, in Games 1 and 3 of the Hawks' conference finals sweep, making 44 saves each time, then heard the United Center fans chant his name after stopping 32 of 33 shots in Game 2 of the Cup finals.

"It's an unbelievable feeling, the way the people react," Niemi said.

Cheers, indeed.

Scotty Bowman laughed off questions about the team's goaltending, saying the goalie to lead Chicago to the Stanley Cup finals was already on the roster. He was right about Antti Niemi. JOSE M. OSORIO

In the middle of traffic, Antti Niemi kept his view clear, rarely losing sight of the puck.

SCOTT STRAZZANTE

The Thrashers watch as Kim Johnsson scores during the Chicago's 5-4 shootout win in February. Injuries slowed Johnsson's contributions. CHRIS SWEDA

PROFILE Dustin Byfuglien

By Philip Hersh

Dustin Byfuglien began the 2010 season as the classic grinder.

That's the guy who works his tail off doing the dirty work on the third or fourth line and hopes it impresses the coach enough to stay in the lineup.

By the day after the first game of the Stanley Cup finals, Byfuglien was the guy having actor Vince Vaughn pick up his dinner tab.

You can be sure the bill ran more than the cost of a grinder, since the Hawks forward and film star were eating at Japonais, an acclaimed Chicago restaurant where one of the chef's sushi specials is $66.

That's probably not the sort of seafood Byfuglien imagined as a reward when he gave up hockey for a year when he was 15 to hunt and fish near his trailer home in far northern Minnesota.

"Yeah, I guess I made a good choice coming back," he told the Tribune's David Haugh.

That conversation took place as Byfuglien was becoming the offensive sensation of the playoffs, moving onto the team's top line with Jonathan Toews and Patrick Kane and scoring in five straight games — he totaled eight goals, with four game-winners — in the second and third rounds of the playoffs.

"He's proving to a lot of people how good he is,"

Kane said.

Byfuglien's reaction was fitting for a person who, despite one gaudy post-goal celebration in the Vancouver series, tends to show off in inverse proportion to his 6 feet 4 inches and 257 pounds.

"When you're playing with those two kids," he said, referring to Kane and Toews, "the puck is going to find you, even when you're not expecting it."

His offense was even more unexpected after having spent most of the previous two months — and first playoff round — filling in for the injured Brian Campbell as a defenseman, the position Byfuglien had played until former Hawks coach Denis Savard moved him up to right wing two seasons ago.

When coach Joel Quenneville returned Big Buff to forward in the second round, the idea was to plant his carcass in front of the net so goalies wouldn't be able to see what slick stuff Kane and Toews would throw at them.

Instead of just creating a mess, Byfuglien also found gems in it, whacking in rebounds and loose pucks in the goalmouth. In the conference final, he also scored on a blistering slap shot from the top of the faceoff circle.

"I always think shooting first instead of making a play," he said.

That's how a grinder becomes a hero.

Big Buff was a lot for most teams to handle, even when they double-teamed him.
CHRIS SWEDA

BRIAN CASSELLA

Whether it was Jonathan Toews and Patrick Sharp taking on Coyotes, Sharp sticking his nose where it belonged vs. the Red Wings or Brent Seabrook introducing a Blue to the ice, the Hawks, one of the most talented teams in the league, were never afraid to mix it up...

SCOTT STRAZZANTE

NUCCIO DINUZZO

... and that included their goalie to start the season, Cristobal Huet, and Colin Fraser, who had a referee between him and a proper introduction to Colorado's Cody McLeod in November.
SCOTT STRAZZANTE

PROFILE **Duncan Keith**

By Philip Hersh

It was ironic yet fitting that everyone truly began to realize what Duncan Keith was made of when some of it came spilling out onto the United Center ice May 23.

Even with big holes in his smile, there are no holes in his game.

Even when he suddenly was missing seven teeth — four bottom, three top —Keith bit off his usual huge piece of the action.

The guy still chewed up a game-high 29 minutes, 2 seconds of ice time, no matter that the puck had made a mess of his mouth during the second period of Game 4 of the conference finals against San Jose. Keith assisted on the tying goal as the Hawks wiped out a 2-0 deficit for the 4-2 victory that sent them to the Cup finals.

"I saw a couple fall out, and I had one in the back of my throat," Keith said. "I could feel it and coughed it out."

Throughout a long season in which Keith, 26, also helped Team Canada win the Olympic gold medal, he never spit the bit.

Played all 82 regular-season games. Led the team with 26 minutes, 35 seconds played per game. Was second on the Hawks — and second among NHL defensemen — with 69 points, with career highs of 14 goals and 55 assists.

Keith had the most points by a Hawks defenseman since Chris Chelios' 72 in 1996.

With occasional flash and stunning consistency, Keith became one of three finalists for the Norris Trophy, given to the league's top defenseman.

"He's not the biggest guy (6 feet 1 inch, 196 pounds) or the strongest guy, but with his speed and a good stick ... he's hard to get around," Calgary scoring machine Jarome Iginla said of Keith after being held without a shot in a 3-1 loss to the Hawks this season.

"He never gives up. He competes very hard."

Hawks management paid tribute to that in early December by giving the Winnipeg native the richest contract in team history at $72 million over 13 years.

Typically, nearly all the attention that day went to the announcement of similar long-term deals for the team's wonderboys, forwards Jonathan Toews and Patrick Kane, who both had been first-round draft picks.

"To be part of this group is pretty special," Keith, a second-round draftee, had said when news of the impending deals surfaced.

Apparently enough to give your eye teeth — and a few others — for

The tooth hurts: Duncan Keith, one of the premiere defenseman in the NHL, looked good whether he was celebrating Kim Johnsson's goal in February or after losing seven teeth vs. San Jose in the conference finals.
CHRIS SWEDA

In February's penultimate game before the Olympic break, Antti Niemi got the start vs. Atlanta, stopping the Thrashers' Niclas Bergfors in the Hawks' 5-4 win. Cristobal Huet was Chicago's entrenched starter at the time. CHRIS SWEDA

Tomas Kopecky, who scored the game winner in Game 1 of the Stanley Cup finals, knows where he's headed vs. the Capitals in what looked like a potential Stanley Cup preview in March. The Hawks lost that game, 4-3 in overtime. JOSE M. OSORIO

Dave Bolland, who emerged as a key contributor during the playoffs, is knocked to the ground vs. St. Louis in February. SCOTT STRAZZANTE

Cristobal Huet cools off with a splash of water in November. By the end of the season, Huet was cooling it on the bench while Antti Niemi started.
NUCCIO DINUZZO

PROFILE **Marian Hossa**

By Philip Hersh

It wasn't cheap, but it still looked like a heck of a deal for the Blackhawks.

They got a guy who had always seemed durable, who had played in the previous two Stanley Cup finals, who was coming off a 40-goal season for Detroit. No Hawk had scored 40 since Tony Amonte in 2000.

And then, three weeks after the Hawks announced July 1 they had signed free-agent forward Marian Hossa to a 12-year deal worth $62.8 million, the team admitted he was damaged goods.

Hossa had rotator cuff issues in his right shoulder that general manager Stan Bowman said were "relatively minor." The next day, the Hawks said Hossa would undergo surgery and miss the first two months of the season.

So maybe they shouldn't have been so quick to let last year's leading scorer, Martin Havlat, leave in free agency.

Those doubts persisted until Hossa scored twice in his first game, Nov. 25 at San Jose.

And the 31-year-old Slovak went on to show that he came with a much wider variety of goods than fans might have thought were in a goal-scorer's package.

He wound up with 24 goals and 27 assists in 54 regular-season games, tied for the league lead with five short-handed goals and tied for the club lead at plus-24. Even given the relentless excellence at both ends by captain Jonathan Toews, it would not be a stretch to call Hossa the team's best two-way player.

"He backchecks so hard, he plays two ways really hard and is great on the forecheck," Patrick Kane said.

Hossa's biggest goal of the season likely was the one that followed his biggest gaffe: a five-minute penalty with the Hawks trailing by a goal late in Game 5 of the first-round playoff series with Nashville.

After Kane sent the game into overtime, Hossa knocked in a rebound soon after his penalty expired, and the Hawks took a 3-2 series lead.

Earlier in the winter, Hossa carried the Slovaks to a fourth-place finish at the Olympics. Three months later, he became the first man to play for three different teams in successive Stanley Cup finals — the first two without hoisting the trophy.

Perhaps those near-misses are why, as linemate Troy Brouwer said after Hossa had two assists in the opener against the Flyers, "he is playing like a man possessed."

Or a man with a lot of surprises in the package.

He got paid, he turned up hurt, he came back and he finally scored in the Stanley Cup finals. Marian Hossa had quite a first season with the Hawks.
SCOTT STRAZZANTE

Patrick Sharp and Kris Versteeg celebrate Sharp's game-winning goal vs. the Kings in March. CHRIS SWEDA

Artie VanBaren triumphantly leads his tribe to the United Center.

Expressions of pride

Photography by Heather Charles

A sea of red and white swirls around the Madhouse on Madison hours before the puck drops inside. The faithful and newcomers revel in Blackhawks memories new and old. They remember when attendance was so low you could stretch out in an aisle. They wear their pride on their faces. Their feet. Their heads. Strangers high-five each other and chant. They make Stanley Cups from pots and pans and dog food dishes. Some paint their cars. Some will tell you they've been waiting for the Hawks to win it all their entire lives.

ABOVE: Jim
Johnson has been
committed to his
beard and the
Blackhawks for a
long time. LEFT:
Yan-Erik Turenne
carries a hand-
some replica of
the real thing.

TOP: Liam Kane, no relation to Patrick. ABOVE: Cindy Rodgers, and while you hope that isn't permanent, you could understand it.

TOP: Like Niemi, Jose Dimas, masked man. ABOVE: Stevan M. Desancic, in full dress before a game vs. San Jose.

TOP: The Hawks mobile. ABOVE: Patrick and Christina Voltz's shoes aren't skates but sure look nice.

TOP: Jim Jensen's collection, right on the button. ABOVE: Michael DePino's Stanley Cup hopes were never overinflated.

REGULAR SEASON STATISTICS

◯ = Hawks leader

NO.	FORWARDS	HT.	WT.	BORN	SHOOTS	CHRIS KUC'S COMMENT
88	Patrick Kane	5' 10"	178	Nov. 19, 1988 in Buffalo	L	*Set career highs with 30 goals and 58 points for the Hawks and helped the United States to a silver medal in the 2010 Olympic Winter Games.*
19	Jonathan Toews	6' 2"	210	April 29, 1988 in Winnipeg, MB	L	*Helped lead Canada to the gold medal in the Olympic Winter Games and a leader on and off the ice as the Hawks' captain.*
10	Patrick Sharp	6' 1"	199	Dec. 27, 1981 in Winnipeg, MB	R	*Established career highs in assists and points as he used his versatility a winger and center to be a steadying influence on the Hawks' offense.*
81	Marian Hossa	6' 1"	210	Jan. 12, 1979 in Slovakia	L	*Missed the first 22 games of the regular season while recovering from shoulder surgery but finished fourth on the Hawks in goals scored.*
32	Kris Versteeg	5' 10"	182	May 13, 1986 in Lethbridge, AB	R	*The flashy winger recorded his second consecutive 20-plus goal season i second season in the NHL to help bolster the Hawks' offensive attack.*
22	Troy Brouwer	6' 2"	214	Aug. 17, 1985 in Vancouver	R	*The big winger came into his own as a scorer in his second full season ar finished with a career-high 22 goals and 18 assists.*
16	Andrew Ladd	6' 2"	200	Dec. 12, 1985 in Maple Ridge, BC	L	*Was a key member of the Hawks' top checking line and also had a career high 17 goals as one of the team's best two-way forwards.*
33	Dustin Byfuglien	6' 4"	257	March 27, 1985 in Minneapolis	R	*Continued to develop into one of the top power forwards in the league as used his size to create havoc in front of opposing goaltenders.*
11	John Madden	5' 11"	190	May 4, 1973 in Toronto	L	*Provided veteran leadership to a young team and was solid at both ends the ice as he reached his fourth Stanley Cup finals.*
82	Tomas Kopecky	6' 3"	203	Feb. 5, 1982 in Slovakia	L	*Registered a career-best 10 goals and 21 points in his first season with th Hawks, including nine goals and nine assists on the road.*
46	Colin Fraser	6' 1"	190	Jan. 28, 1985 in Sicamous, BC	L	*Notched a career-high seven goals and 12 assists, including five goals in final three games of the regular season. Also was a career-best plus-6.*
36	Dave Bolland	6' 0"	181	June 5, 1986 in Mimico, ON	R	*Missed half the season after undergoing back surgery but returned to he the Hawks down the stretch of the regular season and into the playoffs.*
55	Ben Eager	6' 2"	230	Jan. 22, 1984 in Ottawa	L	*Combined physical play with offensive skills to record a career-high 16 p (seven goals) and finished a plus-9 while helping protect teammates.*
29	Bryan Bickell	6' 4"	223	March 9, 1986 Bowmanville, ON	L	*One of the Hawks' top prospects at the winger position, added some size skill to the lineup when called upon during the regular and postseason.*
37	Adam Burish	6' 0"	189	Jan. 6, 1983 Madison, WI	R	*The high-energy forward was limited to 13 regular-season games after suffering a serious knee injury during the preseason and undergoing sur*

NO.	DEFENSEMEN	HT.	WT.	BORN	SHOOTS	CHRIS KUC'S COMMENT
2	Duncan Keith	6' 1"	196	July 16, 1983 in Winnipeg, MB	L	*Recorded career-bests in goals and assists as he elevated his game to a higher level to become one of the NHL's premier defensemen.*
51	Brian Campbell	6' 0"	189	May 23, 1979 in Strathroy, ON	L	*Second among Hawks defensemen with seven goals and 31 assists befor suffering an injury and missing the final 14 games of the regular season.*
7	Brent Seabrook	6' 3"	218	April 20, 1985 in Richmond, BC	R	*Paired with Duncan Keith to form one of the NHL's top defensive pairings earned a gold medal at the Olympic Winter Games playing for Canada.*
4	Niklas Hjalmarsson	6' 3"	205	June 6, 1987 in Sweden	L	*In his first full NHL season, the Eskjo, Sweden, native developed into a to defender with a knack for delivering big hits and clearing the Hawks' zor*
5	Brent Sopel	6' 1"	201	Jan. 7, 1977 in Calgary, AB	R	*Put his body on the line to block opponents' shots and help anchor a stro Hawks defense to reach the Stanley Cup finals for the first time in his ca*
6	Jordan Hendry	6' 0"	197	Feb. 23, 1984 in Lanigan, SK	L	*Went from being a part-time player to emerging into a vital cog for the d with steady play along the blue line down the stretch and into the playof*

TEAM TOTALS

(NOTE: Team totals include some statistics from players not listed here.)

NO.	GOALIES	HT.	WT.	BORN	CATCHES	CHRIS KUC'S COMMENT
31	Antti Niemi	6' 2"	210	Aug. 29, 1983 in Finland	L	*Went from a relative unknown to seize the Hawks' starting goaltender jo training camp and finished third in the NHL with seven shutouts.*
39	Cristobal Huet	6' 1"	205	Sept. 3, 1975 in France	L	*Began the season as the Hawks' No. 1 goaltender and recorded a career- 26 victories before being replaced by Antti Niemi for the postseason.*

TEAM TOTALS

G	A	POINTS	+/-	PIM	PP	SH	GW	OT	SHOTS	SHOT%	ICE TIME PER GAME	SHOTS	GOALS
30	58	88	16	20	9	0	6	0	261	11.5%	19:11	15	4
25	43	68	22	47	9	1	3	0	202	12.4%	20:00	14	8
25	41	66	24	28	4	2	4	1	266	9.4%	18:07	10	2
24	27	51	24	18	2	5	2	0	199	12.1%	18:43	5	2
20	24	44	8	35	4	3	4	1	184	10.9%	15:43	5	2
22	18	40	9	66	7	1	7	1	116	19.0%	16:22	5	1
17	21	38	2	67	0	0	1	0	148	11.5%	13:41	4	1
17	17	34	-7	94	6	0	3	1	211	8.1%	16:25	3	0
10	13	23	-2	12	0	0	0	0	127	7.9%	15:24	2	0
10	11	21	0	28	1	0	2	0	95	10.5%	9:28	3	1
7	12	19	6	44	0	0	0	0	92	7.6%	9:35	0	0
6	10	16	5	28	1	0	0	0	52	11.5%	17:21	1	0
7	9	16	9	120	0	0	2	0	68	10.3%	8:19	0	0
3	1	4	4	5	0	0	1	0	20	15.0%	9:35	0	0
1	3	4	2	14	0	0	0	0	9	11.1%	8:46	0	0

G	A	POINTS	+/-	PIM	PP	SH	GW	OT	SHOTS	SHOT%	ICE TIME PER GAME	SHOTS	GOALS
14	55	69	21	51	3	1	1	0	213	6.6%	26:35	0	0
7	31	38	18	18	3	0	2	0	131	5.3%	23:12	0	0
4	26	30	20	59	0	0	2	2	129	3.1%	23:13	1	1
2	15	17	9	20	0	0	1	0	62	3.2%	19:39	0	0
1	7	8	3	34	0	0	0	0	48	2.1%	14:51	0	0
2	6	8	5	10	0	0	1	0	42	4.8%	11:51	0	0
262	**463**	**725**		**904**	**52**	**13**	**43**	**6**	**2,798**	**9.3%**		**69**	**22**

GS	W	L	OL	GA	GAA	SHOTS	SAVES	SAVE %	SO	G	A	PTS.	PIM	W-L	SAVE %
35	26	7	4	82	2.25	936	854	.912	7	0	1	1	0	6-2	.813
46	26	14	4	114	2.50	1,083	969	.895	4	0	0	0	4	3-4	.658
81	**52**	**21**	**8**	**199**	**2.40**	**2,054**	**1,855**	**.903**	**11**	**0**	**1**	**1**	**4**	**9-6**	**.813**

The Hawks saluted the United Center crowd after clinching their first conference championship since 1993 with a sweep of San Jose. NUCCIO DiNUZZO

Cup Playoffs

Nashville Predators

Conference Quarterfinal

Patrick Kane's goal in Game 2 sealed the Hawks' 2-0 win over the Predators in the first round.
SCOTT STRAZZANTE

A gritty start to the playoffs

By Brian Hamilton

As the Blackhawks' 2010 postseason run began, expectation and anticipation swelled inside and outside the locker room.

A year earlier, for all the burgeoning talent on the roster, the Hawks were postseason newbies and not expected to roil the established order just yet.

By April 16, 2010, when they hosted the Nashville Predators for Game 1 of the first round of the Stanley Cup playoffs, they basically had become the established order.

The Hawks had been a fashionable pick for the Cup all season. They bolted to 112 points in the regular season and the second seed in the Western Conference. The thought of hoisting the Cup for the first time since 1961 seemed entirely plausible, so the pressure accordingly increased and the players accordingly defused the hype.

"Last year we didn't care what anybody said about us," captain Jonathan Toews said in advance of the playoffs. "Every critic seemed to pick Calgary and Vancouver over us. Whatever is said about us is just going to end up water off a duck's back. We're confident as a team. That's all that really matters."

Then the postseason actually began and, at a minimum, it raised a bit of doubt about the first three rounds being mere prelude to a coronation. The Hawks defeated the Predators in a gritty six games to move on to the conference semifinals, but not before having to relearn, essentially, that talent and reputation are trap doors to nowhere in the postseason.

The Predators, for certain, were unimpressed. The United Center was at its full-throated best for Game 1, and the Hawks even carried a lead into the final 20 minutes. But the visitors stunned the crowd into deathly silence with a 4-1 victory thanks to a pair of third-period goals by former Blackhawk J.P. Dumont.

A desperately needed recovery took place in Game 2 with a 2-0 victory, as Antti Niemi recorded the Hawks' first postseason shutout since 1996.

But when the series shifted to Nashville, it shifted right back to a grimy slog, which the Predators preferred. A 4-1 loss in Game 3 put the Hawks on notice.

Predators defenseman Shea Weber crunched Patrick Kane along the boards just more than a minute into the game, and Nashville finished with a 32-18 advantage in hits.

"We're not happy about that," Toews said after the loss. "We knew they were going to be better and playing with more energy in their own building, and we just didn't prepare and expect that enough."

That game turned into a bit of a reckoning. Defenseman Brian Campbell, out with a broken collarbone since getting boarded by Alex Ovechkin on March 14, returned for Game 4. The lineup was shuffled, with the infusion of Adam Burish and Bryan Bickell. The spark was lit.

And the Blackhawks won three in a row to close out the series, including the miraculous finish to Game 5, which may have saved the season. Trailing by a goal in the waning seconds, facing a possible elimination game in Nashville in Game 6 and with Marian Hossa serving a five-minute boarding penalty, Kane seized the big stage.

A horrendous turnover by the Predators' Martin Erat deep in the Nashville zone set up a sequence in which Kane scored a short-handed goal with 13.6

The six-game series was hardly a cakewalk, and in the end, that may have benefitted the Blackhawks more than they realized.

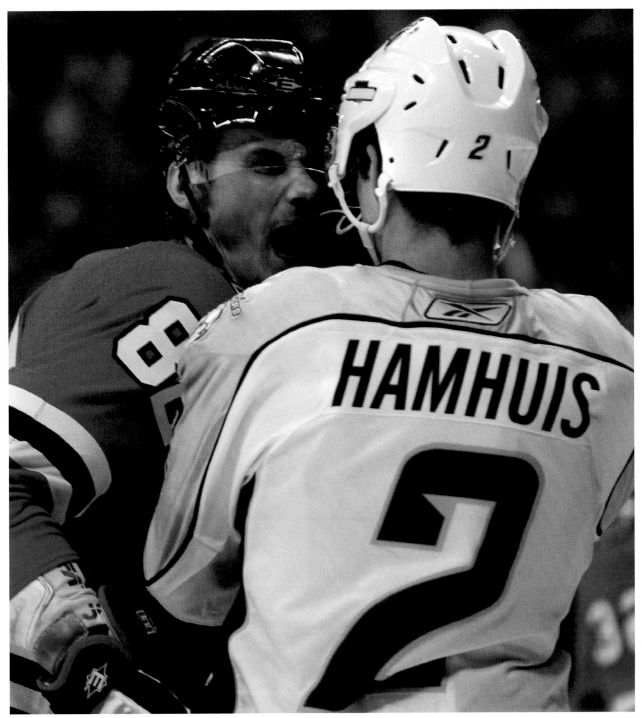

Tomas Kopecky takes no chances that Nashville's Dan Hamhuis didn't get the message. SCOTT STRAZZANTE

seconds left to make it 4-4 and send the game into overtime. Then Hossa jumped out of the box and scored 4:07 into overtime for a raucously improbable victory that rattled the United Center to its foundation.

"I don't even remember the game, to be honest," Kane said. "I just remember us winning. From death to the door opening is a really good feeling."

A 5-3 win in Game 6 in Nashville sent the Hawks into the second round in consecutive seasons for the first time since 1995-96. It was hardly a cakewalk, and in the end, that may have benefitted the Blackhawks more than they realized.

"That was a tough series right from the puck drop of Game 1 until that last buzzer," forward Patrick Sharp said. "We knew it wasn't going to be easy. They have a heck of a team over there. What a series."

Tomas Kopecky's goal at 16:24 of the second period gave the Hawks a 3-1 lead in Game 5, a game Chicago would win 5-4 in overtime. NUCCIO DiNUZZO

Between them, the Hawks and Predators scored seven goals in the first period of Game 6 of the series. Jonathan Toews scored the last one for the Hawks, giving them a 4-3 lead. They won the game 5-3 and the series in six games. NUCCIO DiNUZZO

Tomas Kopecky and Jordan Hendry surround Nashville's Jordan Tootoo in Game 1, won by Nashville. BRIAN CASSELLA

Somewhere between his mobbing teammates and the crowd behind the glass is Marian Hossa, whose goal in overtime gave the Hawks the win in Game 5 and a 3-2 series lead over Nashville. NUCCIO DiNUZZO

Vancouver Canucks

Conference Semifinal

After another series-opening loss, the Hawks rebounded, including Kris Versteeg's goal in the third period to clinch Chicago's Game 2 win vs. Vancouver. NUCCIO DiNUZZO

Making them lose composure

By Brian Hamilton

As the Blackhawks awaited their Western Conference semifinal series against Vancouver, Dustin Byfuglien tugged off his practice sweater in the United Center dressing room.

He had been the 257-pound burr in the Canucks' side a year before, and he had just been switched back to forward for this occasion. Some 50 hours before the series began, before a single second had ticked off the clock in the second round of the postseason, Byfuglien already had been deemed public enemy No. 33 by puck-addled brains across the border.

"It's just how it is," Byfuglien said. "Looking forward to getting back there and creating some ruckus again."

Ruckus was one way to describe what would become a colorfully tense, thoroughly kinetic and entertainingly barb-filled series between two clubs that had grown into bitter rivals over the course of two seasons. The Hawks had vanquished the Canucks the year before in six games, and they repeated that feat in 2010 as rats, clowns and spot-pickers abounded.

The Canucks went out of their way to downplay the Byfuglien effect, with coach Alain Vigneault not so subtly mispronouncing the burly winger's surname before the series began. Then Byfuglien promptly piled up four goals and two assists, including his first career postseason hat trick in Game 3.

The sedate Sedin twins of the Canucks' top line maintained that they would not be shaken by the antics of the Hawks' checking line. Then they were immediately Rat-tled. Hawks center Dave Bolland — nicknamed the Rat — got under the twins' skin

> **All the chatter overshadowed one conclusion: The Blackhawks emerged from the series playing precisely the brand of hockey that wins Stanley Cups.**

and induced them into wildly uncharacteristic stays in the penalty box.

The contributions of Adam Burish, the Hawks' chief antagonist, included hurling epithets at Canucks winger Alex Burrows from the bench, labeling the Canucks "clowns" and defenseman Shane O'Brien a "spot-picker" to add fuel to the already flaming cauldron.

But all the chatter overshadowed one conclusion: The Blackhawks emerged from the series playing precisely the brand of hockey that wins Stanley Cups.

Not so in Game 1, when the Canucks wiped them off the United Center ice 5-1. Goalie Antti Niemi was pulled to start the third period, and coach Joel Quenneville issued this conclusion afterward: "We can't be happy in any respect with what took place tonight."

At that moment, the grind-it-out philosophy that took hold in the first round re-emerged in the second.

The Hawks mounted a third-period comeback to win Game 2 on Kris Versteeg's late goal. They began to unravel the Canucks in Game 3 behind Byfuglien's effort and then unglued Vancouver entirely in Game 4 as the Canucks took eight penalties that led to four power-play goals, including three by Jonathan Toews, in a stunning 7-4 loss.

"We lost our composure again," Canucks goalie Roberto Luongo said. "I don't know why. We talked about it. We were all on the same page before the game started and … I don't know."

So befuddled was Luongo that he shaved the traditional playoff beard for Game 5. It was a tactic that worked for a night, as the Hawks blew a chance to advance in a lackluster 4-1 loss. But that

Dustin Byfuglien lays out to catch Vancouver's Sami Salo in Game 1 vs. Vancouver. CHRIS SWEDA

merely sent them to their home away from home: anywhere but the United Center.

The Hawks clinched the series in Game 6 at Vancouver, an emphatic 5-1 victory that propelled them to back-to-back conference finals for the first time since 1989-90, on the strength of outscoring the Canucks 17-7 in the three games at GM Place.

Waiting in the wings were the San Jose Sharks, the only team in the West to accumulate more points than the Hawks in the regular season. It was to be the true heavyweight battle that, given the topsy-turvy results in the East, most felt was the unofficial Stanley Cup final.

"When it's a long season like this, sometimes it's nice to get a couple of days off, especially at home, and sit back and kind of watch," winger Patrick Kane said. "For them, hopefully, the layoff kind of creates some rustiness for the next series, and the team going in against them obviously will be more in shape and game-ready."

They'll be here all night, ladies and gentlemen:
Adam Burish and Ben Eager give the Canucks
the business from the bench. SCOTT STRAZZANTE

Vancouver's Alex Burrows (14) and
Daniel Sedin (22) have a wall of Hawks
behind them, cornerstoned by
Antti Niemi. BRIAN CASSELLA

TOP: Dustin Byfuglien gives Alex Burrows a shove to the ice in the deciding Game 6 against Vancouver. SCOTT STRAZZANTE

RIGHT: Antti Niemi looks to the crowd in Game 1 vs. Vancouver, a game in which Niemi would give up five goals and be pulled for Cristobal Huet. NUCCIO DiNUZZO

FACING PAGE: Vancouver goalie Robert Luongo, rattled again, can only stare at Jonathan Toews after giving up another goal to Chicago. BRIAN CASSELLA

San Jose Sharks

Conference Final

Antti Niemi makes one of his 44 saves during Game 1 of the Western Conference finals vs. San Jose.
BRIAN CASSELLA

The not-so-easy four-game sweep

By Brian Hamilton

At the end of it, with the light suddenly reappearing on the horizon of an interminable, agonizing, 49-year wait, Jonathan Toews wanted nothing to do with the shiny object to his left.

There sat the Clarence S. Campbell Bowl, signifying the Blackhawks' Western Conference championship won in an unlikely, closer-than-it-sounded sweep of the San Jose Sharks. Bowing to a bit of superstition and a bit of symbolism, the captain tucked his hands behind his sweater and barely cast a glance at the glimmering trophy.

The Hawks had a much more significant prize in mind.

They could think bigger because Dustin Byfuglien and Dave Bolland continued their rides as unlikely postseason heroes, the former scoring his third and fourth game-winning goals of the postseason and the latter continuing to wreak havoc on the psyches of top lines, this time antagonizing the Sharks' Joe Thornton to distraction.

They did so with Antti Niemi, the postseason neophyte, coming up with two 44-save games in the conference finals to stymie one of the most potent offenses in the league, barely demonstrating a glint of emotion in doing so.

There was Toews, riding a massive 13-game points streak into the Stanley Cup finals and suddenly hearing his name mentioned with luminaries such as Sakic and Yzerman, all at the ripe old age of 22.

And there was Duncan Keith, short seven teeth thanks to a puck to the mouth in Game 4, nonetheless skating back onto the ice and assisting on the game-tying goal in the series clincher.

The mood circulating through the dressing room was one of subdued satisfaction, appreciative of taking one more step than they did the previous season.

"They didn't say a whole lot when I came off because they didn't want to scare me about the way it looked," Keith said. "No stitches. They just stuck a bunch of needles in there and froze it all up. Obviously, it feels a lot better when we win."

In that context, plenty of good feelings had been going around since the middle of the previous round, when it was clear that the Hawks had uncovered the correct formula for postseason success. And though the games were indeed tight against the Sharks, the Western Conference final represented the Hawks' full ascension to prohibitive Stanley Cup favorites.

They started the conference finals on the road, thanks to the Sharks' 113 regular-season points to their 112, and it mattered not at all. Niemi made 44 saves in a 2-1 win in Game 1, the first time in three tries the Hawks had won a series opener.

Then came a 4-2 victory in Game 2, an NHL-record-tying seventh straight playoff road win. By then, the Hawks' antics had worn on the Sharks, with Thornton viciously slashing Bolland on a faceoff late in the game.

"They're just getting frustrated, and they can't take it," Bolland said afterward.

But there was one more mental puzzle to solve: the Hawks' confounding struggles at home, which prompted a bit of mental gymnastics entering Game 3. The team checked into a hotel after the morning skate, aiming to simulate a road atmosphere in the run-up to the game.

"There's no distractions, you get away from everything that could be a distraction, and it seems like it's boded well for us on the road and we're winning games there," winger Patrick Kane said.

The inn thing to do was the right thing to do,

Dustin Byfuglien is ready to celebrate after scoring the goal that sent the Hawks to the Stanley Cup finals for the first time since 1993. NUCCIO DiNUZZO

as Byfuglien scored in overtime for a 3-2 victory in Game 3 and a commanding 3-0 series lead.

What seemed increasingly certain with every win in the series was now almost a foregone conclusion, and the Hawks wasted no time completing the sweep with a 4-2 decision in Game 4.

The mood circulating through the dressing room afterward was one of subdued satisfaction, appreciative of taking one more step than they had the previous season — when the Red Wings ousted them in the conference finals — but aware of the bigger prize at hand.

So with no Cup wins since 1961 and no Cup finals visits since 1992, Toews warily approached the Campbell bowl. He and alternate captain Patrick Sharp had discussed the plan before the game, and they agreed: The Western Conference champion hats would be souvenir enough for the night.

"Caught my eye there," Toews said of the trophy. "Kind of shiny. Didn't need to touch it."

Said Sharp: "Johnny and I talked and thought it was best to just leave that one there. We're proud of being Western Conference champions. It's not easy. But we've got our eyes on the bigger trophy."

RIGHT: Kris Versteeg was in the scrum but the goal past San Jose's Evgeni Nabokov in Game 4 was credited to Brent Seabrook.
NUCCIO DiNUZZO

BELOW: Andrew Ladd checks the Sharks' Joe Thornton in Game 3.
SCOTT STRAZZANTE

FACING PAGE: Dustin Byfuglien catches his balance and his breath on the cross bar during a stop in play of Game 1. NUCCIO DiNUZZO.

As Dave Bolland celebrates his third period goal in Game 3, actors Kevin James and Vince Vaughn (left) pound the glass with the rest of the United Center faithful. SCOTT STRAZZANTE

LEFT: Adam Burish and Kris Versteeg join Jonathan Toews to celebrate with Dustin Byfuglien after Byfuglien's game-winning goal in overtime of Game 3.
BRIAN CASSELLA

You've seen that look before: Dustin Byfuglien and the Hawks skate into the Stanley Cup finals after sweeping San Jose. NUCCIO DiNUZZO

Philadelphia Flyers

Stanley Cup Final

After taking his turn, Jonathan Toews appears ready to hand off to Brent Sopel. But Marian Hossa (81), in his third straight Stanley Cup finals, followed the Hawks' captain. For the first time, Hossa felt the weight of the Cup in joy, not agony.
NUCCIO DINUZZO

Patrick Kane scores one of the Hawks' seven goals — this one against Brian Boucher, after Michael Leighton had been pulled for the second time in the Stanley Cup finals — in Chicago's 7-4 win in Game 5.
BRIAN CASSELLA

After 49 years, the wait is lifted

By David Haugh

Spontaneously, a small pocket of fans in red in a Wachovia Center once full of orange started the chant.

"Thank you, Q! Thank you, Q!"

Coach Joel Quenneville just smiled when asked to sum up his emotions after leading the Blackhawks to their first Stanley Cup title since 1961. "You live for this," Quenneville said. "I'm proud of this team. But give the Flyers credit. ... They kept coming. The building was loud. That was one heck of a series."

Indeed.

Game 6: Kane to the rescue

In the Hawks dressing room after the third period, fresh after they had blown a 3-2 lead to the Flyers by allowing the tying goal with 3 minutes 59 seconds left, nobody panicked. Nobody yelled. Nobody screamed. Nobody doubted.

But everybody looked around the room.

"We just said someone has to get that feeling, someone has to be the hero," captain Jonathan Toews recalled.

Fittingly for the franchise, that someone was Patrick Kane.

At the 4:06 mark of overtime in Game 6, Kane grabbed the puck, flung it toward the net and watched it zip past Flyers goalie Michael Leighton. Officials reviewed the goal, which found the far side of the net. But by the time they had confirmed it, Kane already had streaked down the ice and thrown his helmet and stick into the air.

"I knew it went in right away," Kane said. "What a feeling. I can't believe it. We just won the Stanley Cup. I can't believe this just happened. ... It's something you dream about, scoring the final goal in the Stanley Cup finals."

In the postgame party on the ice, teammates mobbed Kane. Friends came out of the stands to join him. Everybody wanted a piece of the man with the mullet.

"Having it be Kaner, he's been awesome all series," said Toews, winner of the Conn Smythe Trophy as playoff MVP. "There's so many great things about winning a Stanley Cup. This is the best feeling you can ever get. I just can't believe it's happened."

It wasn't easy. The tying goal that delayed the popping of corks came when Scott Hartnell banged in a goal that came off Ville Leino's stick and bounced off Marian Hossa's skate and past Antti Niemi.

Turns out that only made the ending more dramatic, and that's when Kane thrives.

"You always want to come through with the pressure on," Kane said. "It's crazy I did."

Game 5: End of the lines

On the way home from Philadelphia after losing Game 4, Quenneville passed out sheets of paper to his staff, general manager Stan Bowman and senior adviser Scotty Bowman. He asked everyone to write down some new line combinations, a brainstorming session that resulted in a torrent too powerful for the Flyers to overcome. The first 10 minutes of the 7-4 victory were as impressive an overall display as the Hawks had put together all season.

"We found energy off shuffling the lines," Hossa said.

In an attempt to wear down Flyers defenseman Chris Pronger, Quenneville separated Kane, Toews and Dustin Byfuglien. Toews skated with Hossa and Tomas Kopecky. Kane joined Andrew Ladd and

Continued on Page 118

Tomas Kopecky, arguably the Hawks' hero in Game 1, gets rough with the Flyers' Dan Carcillo in Game 2. SCOTT STRAZZANTE

Patrick Sharp on the second line, while Byfuglien skated with Kris Versteeg and Dave Bolland.

Afterward, Kane was asked why Byfuglien had responded so well with two goals, two assists and nine hits.

"He got rid of us and started performing," Kane deadpanned.

The attack mentality was obvious from the puck drop. Brent Seabrook, on a power play with Hartnell in the box, drilled home a goal from the left circle at the 12:17 mark. To add to the delight of a home crowd that never had sounded louder, the goal bounced off the skate of Pronger — Public Enemy No. 1 in Cook County.

Pronger picked a bad night to go minus-5. As he was sent to the penalty box at 15:18 of the second period for hooking Kane, the crowd showed its appreciation.

"Pronger sucks! Pronger sucks!" fans chanted.

Clearly, Hawks fans were sick of seeing Pronger. They would not see him in Chicago again.

Game 4: Nicked by Hjalmarsson's mistakes

Pressure called the Wachovia Center, and nobody with an Indianhead on his sweater picked up until the third period. Had the Hawks played with the desperation throughout the entire game they displayed after falling behind 4-1, they might have returned to Chicago with a chance to clinch in Game 5. Instead they turned the puck over in their own zone, committed careless penalties out of frustration and watched again as their top line bottomed out at the worst possible time.

Whatever Quenneville tried to get his team mentally ready, it didn't work. It took only 36 seconds into the game for the Hawks to show a lack of focus when Andrew Ladd was whistled for interference, the first of seven Hawks penalties.

It got worse when Mike Richards stole the puck from Niklas Hjalmarsson in his own zone and whipped a wicked backhand past Niemi at 4:35 to make it 1-0.

Hjalmarsson committed another bad turnover later in the period when his feeble attempt to clear after a shot by Claude Giroux was intercepted by Matt Carle, who converted past Niemi at the 14:48 mark to make it 2-0.

By then it was clear one team had come focused and ready, and one team hadn't.

Quenneville tried sending a subtle message by inserting a healthy Ladd and Nick Boynton for Adam Burish and Jordan Hendry, respectively, in the Blackhawks' lineup. They weren't major moves, but they were attention-getters.

Thing is, the Hawks had to be paying attention, and it appeared more than a few didn't.

Game 3: Too shifty in OT loss

With at least two Hawks running off the ice at the end of their shift, the Flyers took advantage of a de facto power-play opportunity, and Giroux scored on a redirection for the game-winner at the 5:59 mark of a 4-3 overtime loss.

The three Hawks left on the ice in front of Niemi — Duncan Keith, Seabrook and Bolland — didn't have a chance. Suddenly, Philly was convinced the Flyers did.

"It shouldn't happen, and we need to be a little smarter," Keith said.

On the road in the Stanley Cup finals is no time for in-game, organizational mistakes and Quenneville took all the responsibility for the botched line change even if his players may have been more at fault.

"I don't want to get too technical and we don't want to point fingers, but when you're trying to match lines, sometimes you're going to be vulnerable to a tough change," Quenneville said. "In a situation like that, I'll take the hit for it."

The Hawks took plenty from the Flyers, who played a more physical game in their own building. They baited the Hawks into bad penalties and scored their first two goals on power plays. At the end of the first period, the ruffian approach even drew Kane into a melee.

Midway through the second period, Kane's helmet got knocked off, and it skidded across the ice. This was a game the Hawks would remember for the way they lost their heads too.

Game 2: Ho-Ho-Hossa delivers the goods

When Hossa pumped his fist and glanced up toward the hockey heavens after scoring the first goal in the Blackhawks' 2-1 victory, he knew.

Every member of the front office who helped sign Hossa to a 12-year, $62.8 million contract knew too. So did everybody from the 300 level to the $2,000 seats behind the glass.

"It's been a long time," Hossa said after his first goal in eight games.

It came at the 17:09 mark of the second period when Hossa knocked home a rebound past Leighton to break a scoreless tie and give his team a much-needed confidence boost.

Hossa hadn't scored since May 5. He had two assists in Game 1 that were key to the opening win

What, them worry? Apparently, after Philadelphia's Scott Hartnell tied Game 6 at 16:01 of the third period, Hawks' fans watching at West End could barely look. E. JASON WAMBSGANS

but, like any goal-scorer, realized that wasn't his main job.

"It bugged me, definitely," Hossa said of his goal drought. "I tried to create offense, but when I shot the puck it didn't want to go in. I tried not to get frustrated, but I did."

Most significantly, the goal rattled Leighton out of the comfort zone he had created for himself. Exactly 28 seconds after Hossa's goal, ex-Flyer Ben Eager shocked the crowd with a wicked wrist shot from the top of the faceoff circle that set off the red light.

While Leighton flinched, Niemi again resembled the postseason hero more than the guy who gave up five goals in Game 1. The most crucial of Niemi's 32 saves may have come with about two minutes left, when he rejected Ville Leino by going low. But there were others. So many others.

The performance prompted the crowd of 22,275 to chant, "Niemi! Niemi!" after he'd survived the final 1:44 when the Flyers pulled their goalie.

"An unbelievable feeling," Niemi said.

Game 1: Kopecky to the rescue

For 18 years, Chicago had waited for the Blackhawks to show up in a Stanley Cup final. What was another 48 minutes?

That's when Tomas Kopecky rewarded a worried United Center crowd of 22,312 with the game-winning goal in a 6-5 victory that was more wide-open and wild than anybody had expected.

Kopecky, who hadn't played since Game 5 of the Vancouver series and was in the lineup only because of an injury to Ladd, beat Brian Boucher after a pretty pass from Versteeg to knock home the winner at 8:25 of the third period.

"Remarkable comeback," Quenneville said of Kopecky's journey.

It represented more of the remarkable playoff timing by Quenneville that every Stanley Cup champion requires. When Quenneville replaced Kopecky in the lineup with Troy Brouwer for Game 6 against the Canucks, Brouwer responded with a key goal that began Brouwer's resurgence, which he continued with two goals in Game 1 of the finals.

Kopecky's goal positively relieved home fans who had begun to wring their hands and helped a Hawks team rediscover the mojo that was missing most of the night.

It was the first time since 1982 that five goals had been scored in the first period of a Stanley Cup final.

"Shootout at the OK Corral," Quenneville said.

Kopecky's goal seemed to settle down Niemi, whose glove save of a Danny Briere shot with 2:04 left typified how solid he was over the final 10 minutes.

Leighton, a former Blackhawk, resembled the guy beaten out in Chicago by Craig Anderson in 2005, giving up five goals on 20 shots. It got so bad that Flyers coach Peter Laviolette finally pulled Leighton in the second period for Boucher, who had been out with a sprained knee since May 10.

"We were lucky to steal that one," Toews admitted.

After the franchise's first Stanley Cup finals victory in 37 years, no apology was necessary.

ABOVE: Philadelphia's Danny Briere was more than a handful for Chicago, particularly Patrick Sharp. NUCCIO DINUZZO

LEFT: Former Flyer Ben Eager is all too in clearing out Philadelphia's Ville Leino and teammate Duncan Keith in the first period of Game 4 at the Wachovia Center. SCOTT STRAZZANTE

ABOVE: The Hawks' Dustin Byfuglien vs. the Flyers' Chris Pronger: A couple of heavyweights battling in the crease. Pronger may have won more battles, but Byfuglien won the war. SCOTT STRAZZANTE

LEFT: While the regular season centered around who should be the starter in goal — Cristobal Huet, Antti Niemi or a goalie to be acquired — the playoffs were clearly Niemi's time. And by the arrival of the Stanley Cup finals, Hawks' fans were pro Antti in every way. BRIAN CASSELLA

TOP: A Hawks fan chugs his championship champagne in Philadelphia.
BRIAN CASSELLA

ABOVE: White Sox fans shared the celebration from U.S. Cellular Field on the night of the clincher. CHRIS SWEDA

LEFT: Outside Joe's Bar, after Game 6, aluminum foil will do just fine.
WILLIAM DESHAZER

From Kaner to Steeger, Patrick passed the Cup to Kris while Andrew Ladd (16) captures the moment. SCOTT STRAZZANTE

The communion of the Cup, where Tomas Kopecky serves, Brian Campbell drinks and Patrick Kane is overfilled with joy. SCOTT STRAZZANTE

One of the greatest traditions in sport: The team photo, with Stanley always the center of attention. SCOTT STRAZZANTE

Big Buff, Dustin Byfuglien, flies along with the Hawks' colors in tow, after Game 6 of the Stanley Cup finals.
SCOTT STRAZZANTE